MADLIBERALS

Stupid Fill-in-the-Blanks
for Smart Bush Haters

MadLiberals

A PARODY BY WILSON "SCOOTER" BUCKLEY III

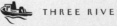 THREE RIVERS PRESS • NEW YORK

ISBN-13: 978-0-307-35107-4
ISBN-10: 0-307-35107-6

Printed in the United States of America

Photograph on page 2 courtesy of AP Images.

Design by Sarah Maya Gubkin

10 9 8 7 6 5 4 3 2 1

First Edition

How to Use This Book

Hey, you're a liberal. You're smart. You already know how to use this book.

But just in case you grew up without this great pastime, here are the rules:

1. One person, you, the MadLiberal, holds the book. Your friends don't get to see the page you're reading.
2. When you see a blank (_____) with a category underneath, call out that category. For example, "I need the name of a small country recently invaded by the United States."
3. The group then gives you a word that fits that category (or, if you want to be quite bold, a word that *sort of* fits that category). You write it in the blank and continue the process.

4. When the page is all filled in, the MadLiberal reads the page out loud.

For those of you who skipped Mrs. Blaisdell's English class, here's a refresher of various parts of speech and other categories:

Verb — an action.
Verb that ends with -ing — an action, like *running*.
Noun — a person, place, or thing.
Adjective — a word that describes something. Vivid words (like *ridiculous*) work the best.
Adverb — a word that modifies a verb; usually ends in -ly, like *stupidly*.
Exclamation — *yikes!*
Members of a profession — *plumbers*, as in Watergate.
Superlative — the extreme degree of comparison of an **adjective** or **adverb**, usually ending in -est, like *luckiest* or *ugliest*.

We're going to assume you're not going to have any trouble with categories like *unindicted coconspirator, dangerous liquid, endangered civil liberty,* or *weapon of mass destruction.*

MadLiberals work best when you follow a few general guidelines:

Be creative: Unusual words often produce funnier results than common ones. If you're asked for a noun, try "salami" or "crossbow" instead of "table" or "chair"; for an adjective, use "bodacious" instead of "pretty," "humongous" instead of "big."

Be political: This gets to the whole point of MadLiberals. For a noun, choose "anthrax" before "pencil"; for a name, try "Osama" or "Condoleezza" instead of "Bob" or "Jane." (Dick is just fine.) Need a verb? How about "impeach"?

On the left-hand page of each spread, you'll find a bonus. It might be the original quote, with a source, or perhaps you'll find the same MadLiberal blanks filled in by a well-known person.

MadLiberals

1. INTELLIGENT DESIGN

Dick...
Laura and I loved doing this.
You and Lynne should try it.
W.

It's obvious that if you teach a kid that he came from a

horse dog zebra _____, he's likely to ___run___
<small>an unusual creature at the zoo</small>   <small>verb</small>

like a _____zebra_____. One of the biggest reasons
<small>that same unusual creature at the zoo</small>

that _secret CIA prison_ scores are down and ___evildoers___
<small>noun</small>   <small>noun (plural)</small>

are up is that Charles Darwin was no _____Gandhi_____.
<small>disgraced religious leader</small>

Science needs to follow the word of _____Loki_____,
<small>character from mythology</small>

not the "theories" of a ___crepuscular___, ___vain___
<small>adjective</small>   <small>adjective</small>

Englishman.

In fact, _baseball players_ from _____France (!)_____
<small>members of a profession</small>   <small>disrespected country that's not as good as the U.S.</small>

are unable to show that _____dogs_____ respond to
<small>type of animals</small>

a clear and unwavering strength of character.
<small>stimulus</small>

Look, if a ___no such thing___ evolved into a person, then I'm
<small>prehistoric creature</small>

as ___bodacious___ as ___Hillary Clinton___.
<small>adjective</small>   <small>well-known Democrat</small>

It's obvious that if you teach a kid that he came from a

_____, he's likely to _____
an unusual creature at the zoo   verb

like a _____. One of the biggest reasons
that same unusual creature at the zoo

that _____ scores are down and _____
noun   noun (plural)

are up is that Charles Darwin was no _____.
disgraced religious leader

Science needs to follow the word of _____,
character from mythology

not the "theories" of a _____, _____
adjective   adjective

Englishman.

In fact, _____ from _____
members of a profession   disrespected country that's not as good as the U.S.

are unable to show that _____ respond to
type of animals

_____.
stimulus

Look, if a _____ evolved into a person, then I'm
prehistoric creature

as _____ as _____.
adjective   well-known Democrat

2. TOP QUOTES FROM GEORGE W.

"Knowing these realities, America must not ignore the threat gathering against us. Facing clear evidence of peril, we cannot wait for the final proof—the smoking gun—that could come in the form of a mushroom cloud."

—President Bush Outlines Iraqi Threat: Remarks by the President on Iraq, Cincinnati Museum Center, October 7, 2002

"America will never seek a permission slip to defend the security of our country."

—State of the Union, January 20, 2004

"Any person, organization, or government that supports, protects, or harbors terrorists is complicit in the murder of the innocent and equally guilty of terrorist crimes."

—Aboard the USS *Abraham Lincoln,* May 1, 2003

"Do I think faith will be an important part of being a good president? Yes, I do."

—Interview, *U.S. News & World Report,* "George W. Bush: Running on His Faith," December 6, 1999

"Every nation, in every region, now has a decision to make. Either you are with us, or you are with the terrorists."

—Address to a Joint Session of Congress and the American People, September 20, 2001

✶   ✶   ✶

America must not ignore the _____ gathering
against us. Facing clear evidence of _____, we
cannot wait for the _____ proof—the smoking
_____—that could come in the form of a _____
cloud.

type of weather

something you're afraid of

adjective

weapon

vegetable

_____ will never seek a permission slip to
_____ the security of our _____.

Country

verb

noun (plural)

Any government that supports, protects, or harbors
_____ is complicit in the _____
of the innocent and equally guilty of _____.

profession (plural)

crime

vacation activity

Do I think _____ will be an important part of
being a _____ president? Yes, I do.

hobby

adjective

Every nation, in every region, now has a decision to make.
Either you are with the _____, or
you are with the _____.

professional sports team

popular religion (practitioners of)*

_____

*E.g., *Protestants, Catholics, Mormons,* etc.

3. WATCHING THE STORE

"**On October 7** the U.S. General Accounting Office (GAO) released a report, "DOD Excess Property: Risk Assessment Needed on Public Sales of Equipment That Could Be Used to Make Biological Agents." According to the Associated Press, using a fake company, congressional investigators were able to use the Internet to buy excess Pentagon lab equipment and protective gear that terrorists could use to make chemical and biological weapons. Fellow shoppers on the Internet site also resold the items to buyers in the Philippines, Malaysia, Egypt, and other countries, the GAO said in a report to the House Government Reform's national security subcommittee. Gregory Kutz, the GAO's director for financial management and assurance, said that they were able to buy $4,100 worth of items, including a biological safety cabinet, a bacteriological incubator, a centrifuge, an evaporator, and chemical and biological protective suits and related gear. He said the original acquisition value of the items purchased was $46,960."

—British American Security Information Council website, www.basicint.org

★ ★ ★

To: _____ _____@yahoo.com
      verb ending in -ing   animal

From: e_____.com
                      weapon (plural)

Subject: Order Confirmation

Dear _____ _____,
      same verb ending in -ing   same animal

Thank you for your recent order of:

- one biological safety _____
                              noun

- one bacteriological _____
                              kitchen appliance

- one set of protective _____
                                  clothing item (plural)

- _____ sets of _____ _____ surgical gloves
       number   color   fabric

- one copy of The _____ *Cookbook,* with
                          biological weapon

   _____
          television chef

- _____ _____ masks
      large number   cartoon character

People who bought these items also bought:

- _____, Widescreen Edition
          James Bond movie

- _____: The Complete First Season
          reality show

Gift card message: Happy _____. Enjoy your trip
                                  holiday

to _____!
          city in U.S.

Note: If shipping to a cave in _____, spider hole in
                                      Islamic country

_____, or cell in _____,
  country invaded by the U.S.   scandal-ridden U.S. prison

please check "No signature required."

4. HOW TO PICK A SUPREME COURT JUSTICE IN FIVE EASY STEPS

"In selecting a nominee, I've sought to find an American of grace, judgment, and unwavering devotion to the Constitution and laws of our country. Harriet Miers is just such a person."
— George W. Bush, Speech from Oval Office, October 3, 2005

"You are the best governor ever—deserving of great respect!"
— Harriet Miers, Note in belated birthday card to George W. Bush, 1997

1. Go through your old _____ cards and find one filled
    _{holiday}

    with the _____ praise. Look for phrases like, "You
    _{superlative}

    are the _____ governor ever—deserving
    _{superlative}

    of great _____," or describing you as
    _{noun (plural)}

    "the most brilliant _____ I ever met!"
    _{job/profession}

2. Look for someone you've known for at least _____ years.
    _{number}

    This will ensure her loyalty and allow you to say things

    like, "I've known this candidate for more than _____
    _{same number}

    years. I know her _____. I know her character."
    _{internal organ}

3. If you want to hide an agenda, there's no better way than to pick a nominee without a _____ paper trail. A
   _{adjective}
   _____ statement like, "I've sought to find an Amer-
   _{adjective}
   ican of grace, judgment, and _____ devotion to the
   _{adjective}
   Constitution and _____ of our country," can
   _{plural noun}
   steer the _____ away from the fact that
   _{disrespected professions}
   your nominee doesn't have any _____ experience.
   _{sport}

4. If your plan starts to turn _____, you can always
   _{flavor}
   blame the _____ Congressional confirma-
   _{adjective}
   tion process and its _____ need for
   _{adjective}
   _____. Obviously, giving them access to
   _{office supply (plural)}
   everything—internal _____ and _____
   _{noun (plural)}   _{holiday}
   cards included—would undermine your ability to receive
   _____ counsel.
   _{adjective}

5. If all else fails, blame the _____.
   _{formerly respected institution now in disrepute}
   You are now free to nominate anyone you want. Treat
   yourself!

5. DEAR MADLIBERALS

PLAY WITH YOURSELF!

Use this handy table to fill in the blanks used on the next page:

_____ psychological diagnosis	_____ insulting adjective
_____ emotion	_____ noun
_____ slang for "prison"	_____ male politician
_____ adjective	_____ body part
_____ pop star	_____ female politician
_____ article of clothing	_____ noun
_____ another article of clothing	_____ emotion
_____ color	_____ article of clothing
_____ noun	_____ animal
_____ body part	_____ adjective
_____ article of clothing	_____ noun

✳   ✳   ✳

Dear MadLiberals,
I've just been invited to a State Dinner, but don't know what to
wear, or how to behave. Can you help?

Signed, _____
                        psychological diagnosis

Dear _____,
_____
same psychological diagnosis

It's understandable that you are _____ about your
_____
emotion

invitation to the _____. It's quite a _____
_____
slang for "prison"   adjective

event and one you should be prepared for.

First of all, this will be a formal evening. You can dress

like _____ on your own time. Now is the time
_____
pop star

to bring out your best _____ and _____;
_____
article of clothing   another article of clothing

a _____ suit is never out of place.
_____
color

The most important thing to remember is that everyone

is naked underneath their _____. Your _____ may
_____   _____
noun   body part

even look nicer than theirs! But it can't hurt if you are wear-

ing your best _____.
_____
article of clothing

Be wary of the _____ international crowd.
_____
insulting adjective

Amazingly, wearing a _____ is considered an insult in many
_____
noun

parts of the world, and should be avoided. When you meet

_____, please don't stare at his _____ and be sure to
_____   _____
male politician   body part

praise _____ on how well her decorative _____ suits her.
_____   _____
female politician   noun

When you see the President, don't get _____; he puts his
_____
emotion

_____ on one leg at a time, just like you. The President
_____
article of clothing

is very fond of cowboy boots made from _____ hide; it is
_____
animal

considered in _____ taste to comment poorly on them. Try
_____
adjective

to find something nice to say about his _____ instead.
_____
noun

6. PAINFUL FOR THE LADIES TO HEAR

What Republican Presidential Candidates Say:

"I know this is painful for the ladies to hear, but if you get married, you have accepted the headship of a man, your husband. Christ is the head of the household and the husband is the head of the wife, and that's the way it is, period."

—Pat Robertson, *700 Club,* January 8, 1992

"The feminist agenda is not about equal rights for women. It is about a socialist, anti-family political movement that encourages women to leave their husbands, kill their children, practice witchcraft, destroy capitalism, and become lesbians."

—Pat Robertson, fund-raising letter, 1992

"Women are less equipped physically to 'stay on course' in the brawling areas of business, commerce, industry, and the professions."

—Pat Buchanan, *San Francisco Chronicle*

I know this is _____ for the _____ to hear,
                  adjective   non-PC word for women
but if you get married, you have accepted the _____
                                                         body part
of a man, your husband. _____ is the head of the
                                   Deity
household and the husband is the head of the _____,
                                                      organization
and that's the way it is, period.

The _____'s agenda is not about _____
            well-known organization   plural noun
for women. It is about a _____, anti-_____
                                 adjective   noun
political movement that encourages women to _____
                                                        verb
their husbands, kill their _____, practice
                                       living thing (plural)
_____, destroy _____, and
   sport traditionally played by men   belief system ending in -ism
become _____.
                oppressed minority group (plural)

Women are less able _____ to " _____ "
                         adverb   sports term or cliché, starting with verb*
in the brawling areas of _____, _____,
                               profession or field   college major
industry, and the professions.

_____

*E.g., *go the extra mile* or *throw a curve ball*

7. WHAT TO WEAR TO A FUNERAL

In January 2005, at a ceremony at Auschwitz to remember the sixtieth anniversary of its liberation, Dick Cheney wore a fur-lined olive drab parka with his name embroidered on the pocket. He was wearing green pants. He also wore brown leather-laced work boots. While his parka had a fur-trimmed hood, he also wore a black knit cap with *Staff 2001* embroidered on it.

Courtesy of AP/Herbert Knosowski

★   ★   ★

In January 2005, at a _____ at _____
                      public event   site of assassination

to remember the anniversary of _____, Dick
                               person assassinated

Cheney wore a _____ with a _____ logo
              article of clothing   sports team

embroidered on the pocket. He was wearing _____ pants
                                                color

and _____ _____-hide _____. While his parka
    color   animal   footwear

had a _____ hood, he also wore a black _____
      adjective   type of hat

with _____ embroidered on it.
     T-shirt slogan

    Cheney carried a _____ lunch box with him.
                     cartoon character

His wife had packed _____, _____,
                    food   beverage

and _____. He refused to eat at the memo-
    kind of fruit

rial _____ after the ceremony.
     type of party

    Upon meeting Vice President Cheney, Jacques Chirac, the

leader of France, said, "*Très chic* _____!"
                                     French name for article of clothing

Cheney's response is classified.

8. NEIL BUSH'S BOGUS CONTRACT

In 2002, the Grace Semiconductor Manufacturing Corporation (GSMC) agreed to pay George W. Bush's brother Neil $2,000,000 for consulting services.

His wife's divorce attorney was amazed by this deal. "You have absolutely no educational background in semiconductors, do you?" he asked. "That's correct," Neil responded.

"I know a lot about business and I've been working in Asia quite a long time," he said, adding, "I feel I've had pretty extensive business interaction over there and that's what I would bring, just general business knowledge."

The China contract details were made public in connection with a contentious divorce proceeding between Neil and Sharon Bush, who were married for 23 years. In the March deposition, Neil Bush admitted to having sex with several women who knocked on the door of his hotel room during a business trip to Hong Kong and Thailand. In response to an attorney's questions, he said he did not know the women, and did not pay them any money.

SOURCE: *Los Angeles Times,* November 27, 2003

* * *

On behalf of the President of Grace _____
                                    <small>noun starting with S</small>

Manufacturing Corporation, I cordially invite you to act as a

_____ to GSMC. Even though you have no back-
<small>job title</small>

ground to speak of in _____, the fact that you
                      <small>same noun (plural)</small>

know a lot about _____ is good enough for us.
                 <small>plural noun</small>

For five years of service we will pay you _____ million
number
dollars, in addition to reimbursements for _____.
plural noun

Your services would include _____ GSMC from
verb ending in -ing
time to time with business _____ and policies; pro-
plural noun
viding us with the _____ information and trends
superlative
of the related _____; and other expertized advices.
plural noun
You would also have to attend board meetings, which happen
_____ times a year, though you would primarily be in charge
number
of bringing _____ and other snacks. Under this con-
fast food item (plural)
tract, you would agree to wear a sandwich board stating your
name and title and _____ around in front of potential
verb
investors. As an additional incentive, when you're in town, we
will provide you with lodging at the _____ _____
adjective noun
Hotel, where you are guaranteed visits by several _____
adjective
women.

Any future legal proceedings that result in your being dis-
owned or otherwise stripped of your last name or political re-
lationships will render this offer null and _____.
adjective

9. THE JUSTICE DEPARTMENT ON DIVERSITY

An internal report that harshly criticized the Justice Department's diversity efforts was edited so heavily when it was posted on the department's Web site two weeks ago that half of its 186 pages, including the summary, were blacked out . . . [the report stated that the Department's efforts were] seriously flawed, specifically in the hiring, promotion, and retention of minority lawyers.

—*New York Times,* October 31, 2003

"By attempting to pigeon-hole and limit diversity into the same old racial and ethnic categories, I believe the court, and certainly the country's university administrators, do not understand how truly diverse we are as a nation. We are a nation of a multitude of views, formed not just by the few race boxes on an application form, which themselves are beginning to appear antiquated as our population intermarries, but by our religions, our places in the economy, our participation in politics, where we live, our interests, and on and on. It is this diversity which makes America strong and which we should never ignore. . . . So the department's diversity program does include outreach efforts aimed at racial and ethnic minorities, including Asian Americans. But it also includes initiatives that benefit all department attorneys. For example, it includes a loan forgiveness program for students burdened with student loans who want to commit to careers in public service."

—Larry Thompson, formerly of the Justice Department, *2003 Federalist Society Address, 17th Annual National Lawyers Convention,* November 14, 2003

✷   ✷   ✷

By attempting to pigeon-hole and limit diversity into the same old racial and ethnic categories, I believe the _____,
government body
and certainly the country's _____ administrators, do
type of school
not understand how _____ diverse we are as a nation.
adverb

We are a nation of a multitude of views formed not just by the few race boxes on a _____ job application
fast-food chain
form, but by our _____ preferences, whether
type of footwear
we like _____ or _____ better, our par-
political radio or TV show   _reality show_
ticipation in _____, where we _____, our
sport   _verb_
favorite kind of _____, and on and on. It is this
alcoholic beverage
diversity which makes America _____ and which
adjective
we should never ignore.

So the department's diversity program does include out-reach efforts aimed at racial and ethnic minorities, including _____ Americans. But it also includes initiatives
minority group
that benefit all minority _____. For
member of profession (plural)
example, it includes a _____ program for students
service offered by a bank
burdened with student loans who want to commit to careers in

_____.
profession

10. "RIGHT BETWEEN THE HEAD," O'REILLY AND FRANKEN

This is what the original Loofah-commentator, Bill O'Reilly, had to say about Al Franken:

> *"What this guy writes and says does not matter to me, other than he insulted me in a forum where I was at a decided disadvantage. You know, he went over his time limit. It was very, very sneaky.*
>
> *"And you know, as I said at the top of the broadcast, somebody calls you a liar to your face, you don't just laugh that off. Okay, that's—that's an insult. In the Old West, that would have got you shot.*
>
> *"See, in the Old West—and I would have loved to have been in the Old West—Al and I would have just had a little—a little shoot-out, you know? We would have went out on Wilshire Avenue, with six-shooters. Now, he's a much smaller target than I am—about four-foot-eleven, but he's wider. And it would have been, you know, Clint Eastwood time. I would have had the serape, would have given my squint, and I would have put a bullet right between his head.*
>
> *"Would have been wrong, would have been wrong. But it was the Old West, and I would not have known any better. So I wouldn't have been accountable because I would not have known any better. Now I do. Now, in 2003, that would have been wrong."*

★   ★   ★

"What _____ writes and _____ does
        male liberal   bodily function, present tense

not matter to me, other than he insulted me in a _____
                                                                              type of room

where I was at a decided disadvantage. You know, he went over

his _____ limit. It was very, very _____.
       noun   insulting adjective

"And you know, as I said at the top of the broadcast, somebody calls you a _____ to your _____, you don't

(noun)   (body part)

just _____ that off. Okay, that's—that's an insult. In

(bodily function)

the _____, that would have got you _____.

(period of history (noun))   (verb, past tense)

"See, in the _____—and I would have

(same period of history (noun))

loved to have been in the _____—_____

(same period of history (noun)) (same male liberal)

and I would have just had a little—a little game of _____,

(game)

you know? We would have went out on _____ with

(famous street)

_____. Now, he's a much smaller

(items used in same period of history (plural noun))

target than I am—about _____-foot-eleven, but he's wider.

(number)

And it would have been, you know, _____ time.

(hawkish politician)

I would have had the _____, would have given my

(part of a uniform)

best _____, and I would have put a _____ right

(rude noise)   (noun)

between his head.

"Would have been wrong, would have been wrong. But it

was the _____, so I wouldn't have been

(same period of history (noun))

accountable because I would not have known any better. Now

I do. Now, that would have been wrong."

11. PRAYER IN SCHOOL

From the U.S. Department of Education

Generally, students may pray in a nondisruptive manner when not engaged in school activities or instruction, and subject to the rules that normally pertain in the applicable setting. Specifically, students in informal settings, such as cafeterias and hallways, may pray and discuss their religious views with each other, subject to the same rules of order as apply to other student activities and speech. Students may also speak to, and attempt to persuade, their peers about religious topics just as they do with regard to political topics. School officials, however, should intercede to stop student speech that constitutes harassment aimed at a student or a group of students.

Students may also participate in before- or after-school events with religious content, such as "see you at the flag pole" gatherings, on the same terms as they may participate in other noncurriculum activities on school premises.

School officials may neither discourage nor encourage participation in such an event.

✴   ✴   ✴

From the U.S. Department of Education

Generally, students may pray in a _____ manner when not
                                    adjective

engaged in school activities or during _____
                                        controversial subject taught in school

class, and subject to the rules that normally pertain. Specifi-

cally, students in _____ settings, such as _____
                    adjective   place in a school (plural)

or _____, may pray and discuss their views on
other place in a school (plural)

the _____ or _____ with each other, sub-
holy book   Greek god

ject to the same rules of order as apply at _____
scandal-tainted prison

and _____. Students may also speak to and at-
presidential vacation spot

tempt to _____ their peers about religious _____
verb   plural noun

just as they do with regard to political topics. _____,
Job at a school (plural)

however, should _____ to stop student speech that con-
verb

stitutes harassment aimed at members of the _____
school club or team

or _____ teachers.
school subject

Students may also participate in before- or after-school

_____ with _____ content, such
activity found in Bible*   noun

as "see you at (the) _____" gatherings, on the same
holy site

terms as they may participate in other noncurriculum activities

on school premises.

School officials may neither discourage nor encourage par-

ticipation in such _____.
same biblical activity

_____

*E.g., *walking on water, talking to a burning bush, ark building,* etc.

12. DUE TO INCREASED SECURITY

PLAY WITH YOURSELF!

Use this handy table to fill in the blanks used on the next page:

plural noun	body part
plural noun	medical device
household item (plural)	personal item
mass transit vehicle	type of weather
animal (plural)	politician's name
plant (plural)	TV show
adjective	type of punishment
type of uniform	same mass transit vehicle (plural)
verb	adjective

ATTENTION PASSENGERS AND _____ :
                                                  plural noun

Due to increased _____ and concerns about homeland
                          plural noun

security, you are no longer allowed to bring _____
                                                    household item (plural)

with you on this _____. _____
                          mass transit vehicle   Animal (plural)

and _____ must be registered in advance with the
            plant (plural)

_____ guard wearing the _____.
      adjective   type of uniform

At any time, we may _____ you and require that you
                              verb

expose your _____ to us. At any time, our _____
                  body part   medical device

may be used to inspect your _____.
                                      personal item

Please do not make comments about _____,
                                                  type of weather

_____, or _____. Doing so could
      politician's name   TV show

subject you to immediate _____.
                                    type of punishment

Thank you for helping us keep our _____
                                              same mass transit vehicle (plural)

safe and _____.
              adjective

13. FOR US OR AGAINST US

In 2003, beloved performing group the Dixie Chicks made the following comment about the foreign policy of the United States, "Just so you know, we're ashamed the president of the United States is from Texas."

They were met with a firestorm of criticism, including being banned from many radio stations.

Or consider this, from the patriot Trent Lott, "How dare Senator Daschle criticize President Bush while we are fighting our war on terrorism, especially when we have troops in the field."

★   ★   ★

As you know, _____ has publicly criticized the
name of music group

government for the War on _____. This just sends
emotion (noun)

the message to our enemies that we're _____. We need
adjective

_____, not divisiveness.
latest horrifying practice of the Bush administration

There are _____ young men and women risking their
adjective

_____ and it borders on treason for someone like
noun (plural)

_____ to say, "Just so you know, we're
name of person in music group

ashamed the president of the United States _____
verb (present tense)

from _____."
place

If you have their album, _____ it!
verb

If you hear them on _____, turn it off!
radio show

If you hear _____ humming the song,
well-known Democrat

_____ him (or her)!
verb

The only way to combat terrorism is to rally against

_____ like this. The _____ of our great nation is
animal (plural)   noun

at stake. Either you are with the members of _____
same music group

or you are with The _____ Singers. The
Republican politician

choice is yours.

14. 5 STEPS TO HANDLING A NATIONAL DISASTER

"We've got a lot of rebuilding to do. First, we're going to save lives and stabilize the situation. And then we're going to help these communities rebuild. The good news is—and it's hard for some to see it now—that out of this chaos is going to come a fantastic Gulf Coast, like it was before. Out of the rubble of Trent Lott's house—he's lost his entire house—there's going to be a fantastic house. And I'm looking forward to sitting on the porch."

—President Bush, during his first visit to the
Gulf Coast following Hurricane Katrina

"It's totally wiped out. . . . It's devastating, it's got to be doubly devastating on the ground."

—President Bush, turning to his aides while surveying Hurricane
Katrina flood damage from *Air Force One,* August 31, 2005

"I don't think anybody anticipated the breach of the levees."

—President Bush, on *Good Morning America,* six days after
repeated warnings from experts about the scope of damage
expected from Hurricane Katrina, September 1, 2005

1. It's important to keep a cool _____ in an emergency.
    _{body part}
    If you get the news while you're _____, on
    _{leisure activity ending in -ing}
    a working vacation, or at a photo op at a local _____,
    _{business}
    it's best to just soldier on. The disaster can wait. Finding
    out how *My Pet* _____ ends cannot.
    _{animal}

2. Deny any knowledge you had of preventing the _____.
   noun

   Use conviction when you say, "I don't think anybody
   anticipated the breach of the _____," and keep
                                    plural noun
   all relevant _____ classified.
                 plural nouns

3. Eventually, you will have to visit the disaster site. Remember, no matter how _____ it looks from afar, it's
                        adjective
   doubly _____ in person. Standing on a _____,
          same adjective   noun
   loosening your _____, and speaking through a
                   article of clothing
   _____ will help.
    cone-shaped object

4. In order to gain perspective, try thinking about how
   the disaster affected your friends. For instance, was
   _____'s _____ destroyed?
    Republican politician   noun
   Promise the country that you will help rebuild it.

5. Disasters are a _____ opportunity for disguising an
                    adjective
   ulterior agenda. For example, this is a great time to start the
   War on _____ or invade _____. A disaster
          Democratic program   country
   relief bill is also a great place to hide an amendment making
   _____ permanent.
    really bad law passed by Bush administration

15. PRESIDENT BUSH'S NOTE TO SELF BEFORE DEBATE

Was President Bush literally channeling Karl Rove in his first debate with John Kerry? That's the latest rumor flooding the Internet, unleashed last week in the wake of an image caught by a television camera during the Miami debate. The image shows a large solid object between Bush's shoulder blades as he leans over the lectern and faces moderator Jim Lehrer.

. . . On several occasions, the president simply stopped speaking for an uncomfortably long time and stared ahead with an odd expression on his face. Was he listening to someone helping him with his response to a question?

SOURCE: Salon.com, October 8, 2004

✶   ✶   ✶

1. Apologizing is for _____. If I don't apologize, it's
   animal (plural)
   like I never bombed _____ in the first place. So
   oil-rich country
   what if there's no link between _____
   country with nuclear capabilities
   and _____, or that _____
   natural disaster (plural)   developing country
   never had any WMDs.

2. If asked about _____ or _____,
   recent scandal   Republican under investigation
   make it sound like by questioning me, they are questioning
   the _____ itself.
   famous document

3. Emphasize how hard everyone at _____,
   federal agency
   _____, and the _____
   corporation with ties to Bush   domestic help (plural noun)*
   at the Crawford Ranch are working. No one is working as
   hard as _____ to help the American
   White House staff member
   _____.
   noun

4. Staring _____, scratching your _____, or
   adverb   body part
   wrinkling your _____ can also communicate a lot.
   body part

5. Remember, _____ can feed me most
   White House staff member
   answers through the microphone I have hidden in my

   _____.
   undergarment

_____
*E.g., *scullery maids, pool boys,* etc.

16. BUDGET CUTS

Newly appointed Secretary of Education Margaret Spellings started on an intolerant note by attacking the PBS children's show *Postcards from Buster,* on her second day in office. On January 25, Spellings chastised PBS for approving an episode of the acclaimed series that featured a young Vermont girl and her two mothers, though the focus of the episode was on maple sugar and Vermont farm life. In a letter to PBS, which the Department of Education partially funds, Spellings expressed her anger with the episode, explaining she feels U.S. families "would not want their young children exposed to the lifestyles portrayed in the episode." Spellings also suggested that PBS return the money used to make the episode.

SOURCES: *New York Times,* "Culture Wars Pull Buster Into Fray," Julie Salamon, January 27, 2005; *Kansas City Star,* "Education Secretary Condemns PBS Show," Ben Fuller (AP), January 27, 2005; TomPaine.com, "Leave No Cartoon Behind," Earl Hadly, January 28, 2005.

Dear _____,

_____<small>Hollywood liberal</small>

Thank you for your _____ expressing your

_____<small>method of communication</small>

concern about our _____ budget cuts for Public

_____<small>adjective</small>

Broadcasting. Cuts had to be made somewhere and, frankly,

we are rather concerned about some of the _____

_____<small>adverb</small>

correct and offensive-to-members-of-_____

_____<small>conservative group</small>

programming, which we find inappropriate.

You'll recall that in a recent episode of _____,

_____<small>PBS program</small>

_____ visited _____ families that

_____<small>character from same program</small> _____<small>number</small>

turned out to be lesbian households. We do not think it is

appropriate to expose _____ to the lifestyles

_____<small>family member (plural)</small>

_____ in shows like this. In fact, PBS should give us

_____<small>verb (past tense)</small>

back the $_____ we gave them to produce this episode.

_____<small>number</small>

We feel that our yearly budget for PBS of $_____

_____<small>number</small>

can be better put toward things like purchasing _____

_____<small>weapon (plural)</small>

for our troops or American _____ for our classrooms.

_____<small>plural noun</small>

Sincerely,

Margaret _____s

_____<small>grade school subject</small>

Secretary of Education

17. LETTER HOME

WASHINGTON—A week after a soldier told Defense Secretary Donald Rumsfeld that troops were scrounging for scrap metal for do-it-yourself armor plating, the Army said Wednesday that it is spending $4.1 billion to armor all military wheeled vehicles in Iraq by June.

The Army and the Pentagon came under sharp attack by Democrats and Republicans on the House and Senate armed services committees and by soldiers' families after a Tennessee Guardsman, Spc. Thomas Wilson, asked Rumsfeld in Kuwait last week why soldiers had to dig through landfills to find armor for vehicles.

SOURCE: *USA Today*, December 15, 2004

✶   ✶   ✶

Dear Mom,

Things here in _____, where I'm currently
_{country at odds with the U.S.}
stationed, are _____. I enjoyed the _____
_{adjective} _{kind of food}
that you sent me last week. I actually ended up attaching the

_____ to my _____ for protec-
_{packaging or part of same food} _{body part}
tion during combat. Equipment is running low. We've been

_____ in the _____ in hopes of
_{verb ending in -ing} _{geographic feature of above country}
finding scraps of _____ for armor, which doesn't always
_{material}
_____ very well, as you might imagine, especially if the
_{verb}
_____ is _____. We've been promised
_{same material} _{adjective}
armored _____, but so far, those haven't
_{form of transportation (plural)}
materialized. I'm wondering if they knew our enemies would

be equipped with _____ and highly explosive
_{weapon (plural)}
_____. In your next care package, I was thinking
_{plural noun}
you could include cans of _____, as that way I
_{canned food}
would have food *and* protection.

Love,

Your son

18. SORRY WE BOMBED YOUR VILLAGE

Pakistan on Saturday condemned a purported CIA airstrike on a border village that officials said unsuccessfully targeted al-Qaeda's second-in-command, and said it was protesting to the U.S. Embassy over the attack that killed at least 17 people.

Citing unidentified American intelligence officials, U.S. news networks reported that CIA-operated Predator drone aircraft carried out the missile strike because al-Zawahri, Osama bin Laden's top lieutenant, was thought to be at a compound in the village or about to arrive.

"Their information was wrong, and our investigations conclude that they acted on false information," said a senior Pakistani intelligence official with direct knowledge of Pakistan's investigations into the attack.

His account was confirmed by a senior government official who said al-Zawahri "was not there." Both officials spoke on condition of anonymity because of the subject's sensitivity.

SOURCE: AP report, January 14, 2006

"Now, it's a regrettable situation, but what else are we supposed to do?"
—Senator Evan Bayh

✸   ✸   ✸

Transcript of Leaflet Dropped over Bombed City

Dear citizens of _____,

                            foreign city

It is regrettable that your village was bombed, but what else were we supposed to do? We thought we had it on pretty good authority that _____'s lieutenant was hiding in

        villain from a James Bond movie

a _____ in your area. _____'s _____'s

   place   Administration official   service profession

_____'s friend, who is from _____ told

  relative   country at odds with the U.S.

_____'s staff member that he was there. We'll

   Republican politician

be the first to admit, we should have looked into it a bit more _____ before _____ the attack. Especially since

   adverb   verb ending in -ing

it turns out he wasn't there the first time we _____

                                         adverb

bombed your village, either. Perhaps you can look at this as a _____ opportunity to _____ tourism

        adjective   verb

and renovate the businesses that were _____.

                                    verb (past tense)

Anyway, we promise to _____ the best intelli-

                             verb

gence gathered by the _____ before we

                      U.S. government agency

bomb you the next time.

Best regards,

_____

conservative commentator

Deputy Director of Public Relations, Department of Defense

19. FIVE WAYS TO STAY SAFE WHILE TRAVELING

PLAY WITH YOURSELF!

Use this handy table to fill in the blanks used on the next page:

ethnic group	mass transportation vehicle
article of clothing	latest disease mentioned in the news
toothpaste manufacturer	body part
patriotic saying	verb ending in -ing
adjective	same mass transportation vehicle
container	popular vacation spot
article of clothing	number
federal agency	superlative
adjective	member of profession (plural)
citizen of country at odds with the U.S.	

1. If you are _____, do your best to fit in anyway.
   <ethnic group>

   Try wearing an expensive _____ and make ample
   <article of clothing>

   use of _____ whitening strips.
   <toothpaste manufacturer>

2. Say "_____" often.
   <patriotic saying>

3. If you see someone carrying a _____ _____
   <adjective> <container>

   or _____, call the _____ immediately.
   <article of clothing> <federal agency>

   Repeat these words: "There's a _____
   <adjective>

   _____ on this
   <citizen of country at odds with the U.S.>

   _____."
   <mass transportation vehicle>

4. If you see someone coughing, he/she probably has

   _____. Ask him/her to cover his/her
   <latest disease mentioned in the news>

   _____ while _____. If possible, exit the
   <body part> <verb ending in -ing>

   _____ and wait for the next one.
   <same mass transportation vehicle>

5. You don't really need to go to _____ anyway.
   <popular vacation spot>

   After all, season number _____ of your favorite reality
   <number>

   TV show, America's _____ _____,
   <superlative> <member of profession (plural)>

   just came out on DVD.

20. CREATE YOUR OWN IRATE OUTBURST BY A RELIGIOUS LEADER

"I think we need to look at the Bible and the Book of Joel. The prophet Joel makes it very clear that God has enmity against those who, quote, 'divide my land.' God considers this land to be his. You read the Bible, he says, 'This is my land.' And for any prime minister of Israel who decides he is going to carve it up and give it away, God says, 'No. This is mine.'

"He was dividing God's land, and I would say woe unto any prime minister of Israel who takes a similar course to appease the EU, the United Nations, or [the] United States of America. God said, 'This land belongs to me, you better leave it alone.' "

—Pat Robertson, *The 700 Club,* January 5, 2006

"I think we need to take a look at _____ and the

book title

Book of _____. The prophet

first name of high-ranking administrative official

_____ makes it very clear that _____ has

same name   character from mythology

enmity against those who, quote, 'divide my _____.'

toy

_____ considers this _____ to be his.

Same character from mythology   same toy

You read _____, he says, 'This is my _____.'

same book title   same toy

And for any _____ of _____

political title   country

who decides he is going to carve it up and give it away,

_____ says, 'No. This is mine.' . . . And

same character from mythology

I would say woe unto any _____ of

political or royal title

_____ who takes a similar course

country at odds with the U.S.

to appease the _____, the

civil rights organization

_____, or the _____.

environmental group   left-wing Democratic group

_____ says, 'This _____

Same character from mythology   same toy

belongs to me, you better leave it alone.' "

21. INJURIES

"As you can possibly see, I have an injury myself—not here at the hospital, but in combat with a cedar. I eventually won. The cedar gave me a little scratch. As a matter of fact, the Colonel asked if I needed first aid when she first saw me. I was able to avoid any major surgical operations here, but thanks for your compassion, Colonel."

—George W. Bush, after visiting with wounded veterans
from the Amputee Care Center of Brooke Army Medical Center,
San Antonio, Texas, January 1, 2006

★   ★   ★

When dealing with an injured soldier, it is essential to show not just sympathy, but empathy. For example, if you are talking to a _____ just back from _____,

military rank · country

someone who bravely risked his life and lost a(n) _____,

appendage

you should try to _____ him up by sharing that you, too,

verb

have been suffering with _____:

minor medical condition

"As you can possibly see, I have an injury myself—not here at the _____, but in combat with a

building

_____. I eventually won. The _____

vegetation · same vegetation

gave me a little _____. As a matter of fact,

physical injury

the _____ asked if I needed a(n) _____

military rank · medical procedure

when she first saw me. I was able to avoid any

_____ here, but thanks for your

major medical procedure

_____, _____."

emotion (noun) · same military rank

22. BECOME A SPEECHWRITER FOR BUSH!

PLAY WITH YOURSELF!

Use this handy table to fill in the blanks used on the next page:

_____ country	_____ adjective
_____ adjective	_____ noun
_____ branch of government	_____ law enforcement organization
_____ adjective	_____ adjective
_____ country	_____ large number
_____ luxury item	_____ period of time
_____ type of tax	_____ imported natural resource
_____ another country	_____ country
_____ name of current enemy	_____ luxury item (plural)
_____ adjective	_____ Greek god
_____ verb (past tense)	_____ scandal-ridden corporation

Ladies and gentlemen of _____, _____
country   adjective

members of the _____, I thank you. As we
branch of government

meet, I would like to remind you that our _____ men
adjective

and women are currently fighting in _____ for
country

our right to free _____ and freedom from paying
luxury item

_____ in _____. The _____
type of tax   another country   name of current enemy (plural)

are on the run. This is a _____ road we are traveling, a
adjective

challenge that should not be misunder_____. And
verb (past tense)

as much as I am _____ about war, if we hold fast to
adjective

our belief in hard work, _____ ownership, and a free
noun

_____ we will see a _____ future. There have
law enforcement organization   adjective

been _____ important accomplishments over the past
large number

_____. The war is being won. _____
period of time   Imported natural resource

is (are) being saved. And soon, the people of _____
country

will enjoy the same _____ as you and I.
luxury item (plural)

May _____ bless you, and may God bless
Greek god

_____.
scandal-ridden corporation

23. PUT A BUSHIE IN YOUR TANK

Former Oil Lobbyist Employed by White House Leaves to Join ExxonMobil

June 15, 2005: *Less than a week after documents revealed that he had repeatedly manipulated government reports to downplay the threat of global warming, Philip Cooney resigned from the White House and accepted a job with the world's largest oil company. ExxonMobil Corp. also happens to be the industry's most strident opponent of global-warming science. Prior to serving as chief of staff on the White House's Council on Environmental Quality, Cooney headed the climate program at the American Petroleum Institute, the trade group for the oil industry. Cooney resigned his government job two days after news broke about his role in editing global warming studies. A White House official insisted that his departure was "completely unrelated" to the scandal and that Cooney just wanted to "spend time with his family." Exxon announced that Cooney will begin work in the fall, heading up communications.*

"Perhaps he won't even realize he's changed jobs," said David Hawkins, director of NRDC's climate center.

SOURCE: National Resources Defense Counsel website, www.nrdc.org

✷   ✷   ✷

_____ *[To be used wherever "noun1" appears]*
noun

Less than _____ after documents revealed that he
period of time

had repeatedly manipulated government _____ to
plural noun

downplay links between _____ and
noun1 (plural)

_____, Philip Cooney resigned from
environmental concern

the White House and accepted a job with the world's largest

_____ company, which also happens to be the indus-
noun1

try's most strident opponent of _____ science.
same environmental concern

Prior to serving as _____ on the White
job position

House's Council on Environmental Quality, Cooney headed

the _____ program at the American Patriotic _____
noun   noun

Institute, the trade group for the _____ industry. Cooney
noun1

resigned his government job two days after news broke about

his role in _____ _____ studies.
verb ending in -ing   same environmental concern

A White House _____ insisted that his departure
job position

was "completely unrelated" to the scandal and that Cooney

just wanted to "_____ with his family." The _____
verb   noun1

company announced that Cooney will begin work in the fall,

heading up the _____ department.
department in a store

24. THE CASE AGAINST THE STRATEGIC PETROLEUM RESERVE

The Strategic Petroleum Reserve has been almost uniformly embraced by politicians and energy economists as one of the best means to protect the nation against oil supply shocks. This study finds little evidence for the proposition that government inventories are necessary to protect the country against supply disruptions. Absent concrete market failures, government intervention in oil markets is unlikely to enhance economic welfare. . . .

The SPR has been tapped only three times, and in each of those instances, the releases were too modest and, with the exception of the 2005 release related to Hurricane Katrina, too late to produce significant benefits. Accordingly, the costs associated with the SPR have been larger than the benefits thus far.

SOURCE: Cato Institute, *Policy Analysis No. 555,* November 21, 2005

★ ★ ★

The Strategic Petroleum Jelly Reserve (SPJR) has been almost

_____ _____ by politicians and
     adverb   verb (past tense)

_____ economists as one of the _____ means
   noun   superlative

to protect the nation against _____. This study
                             embarrassing medical condition

finds _____ evidence for the proposition that govern-
           adjective

ment _____ are necessary to
       alternative healer or health practitioner (plural)

protect our _____ against supply disruptions.
            type of institution

Absent _____ market failures, _____
        adjective   international aid group

intervention in petroleum jelly markets is unlikely to enhance

economic _____. . . .
           a virtue

    The SPJR has been tapped only _____ times, and in
                                 number

each of those instances, the releases were too _____
                                    adjective

and, with the exception of the _____ release related
                           year

to the _____ epidemic, too late to prevent
      sexually transmitted disease

significant _____. Accordingly, the costs asso-
           common drug side-effect

ciated with the SPJR have been _____ than the
                           comparative adjective*

benefits thus far.

_____
*E.g., *sillier, cheesier,* etc.

25. BILL O'REILLY: UMPIRE

In his book *The O'Reilly Factor,* Bill O'Reilly describes his political affiliation this way: "You might be wondering whether I'm conservative, liberal, libertarian, or exactly what. . . . See, I don't want to fit any of those labels, because I believe that the truth doesn't have labels. When I see corruption, I try to expose it. When I see exploitation, I try to fight it. That's my political position."

✭   ✭   ✭

NEW YORK—2009: Faced with a scandal of ＿＿＿＿＿＿ pro-
_{adjective} portions, Major League Baseball today announced that after

considering ＿＿＿＿＿＿＿＿＿＿＿＿, ＿＿＿＿＿＿＿＿＿＿＿＿,
_{supreme court justice}   _{indicted business person}

and ＿＿＿＿＿＿＿＿＿, they have chosen TV ＿＿＿＿＿＿＿
_{sexy pop singer}   _{noun}

Bill O'Reilly to become Chief Umpire.

"I am very ＿＿＿＿＿＿＿ to accept this very traditional
_{emotion}

and popular appointment," said O'Reilly. "I believe that the

truth doesn't have ＿＿＿＿＿＿＿＿＿＿＿＿＿."
_{baseball term (plural noun)}

In his first game at Fenway Park, with ＿＿＿＿＿＿ strikes
_{number}

and ＿＿＿＿＿＿ balls on the batter, O'Reilly walked to the
_{number}

stands and ejected ＿＿＿＿＿＿＿＿＿＿, who was seated in the
_{left-wing celebrity}

front row, just to the left of ＿＿＿＿＿＿＿＿＿＿＿＿＿＿.
_{senator from Massachusetts}

"S/he was way outside the mainstream!" said O'Reilly.

After a close call at the plate was disputed by the manager

of the visiting ＿＿＿＿＿＿＿ ＿＿＿＿＿＿＿—ers O'Reilly took
_{blue state}   _{liberal cause}

out a loofah sponge and waved it ＿＿＿＿＿＿＿＿ close to the
_{adverb}

manager's ＿＿＿＿. Commissioner of Baseball ＿＿＿＿＿＿＿
_{body part}   _{White House staffer}

called O'Reilly's response a ＿＿＿＿＿＿ act, in the best tradi-
_{adjective}

tion of the ＿＿＿＿＿＿ American game of baseball.
_{adjective}

26. ANN COULTER

"The ethic of conservation is the explicit abnegation of man's dominion over the Earth. The lower species are here for our use. God said so: Go forth, be fruitful, multiply, and rape the planet—it's yours. That's our job: drilling, mining and stripping. Sweaters are the anti-Biblical view. Big gas-guzzling cars with phones and CD players and wet bars—that's the Biblical view."

—Ann Coulter, *The Jewish World Review,* October 13, 2000

"I have to say I'm all for public flogging. One type of criminal that a public humiliation might work particularly well with are the juvenile delinquents, a lot of whom consider it a badge of honor to be sent to juvenile detention. And it might not be such a cool thing in the 'hood to be flogged publicly."

—Ann Coulter, MSNBC, March 22, 1997

"The ethic of conservation is the explicit abnegation of man's

dominion over _____. The _____ species are
                  animal (plural)   adjective

here for our use. God said so: Go forth, be _____ and
                                                 adjective

multiply, and rape the _____—they're yours.
                          same animal (plural)

That's our job: drilling, _____, and stripping.
                              verb ending in -ing

_____ are the anti-Biblical view. Big gas-
   Article of clothing (plural)

guzzling _____ with phones and CD
             mode of transportation (plural)

players and wet bars—that's the Biblical view."

"I have to say I'm all for _____.
                                type of punishment

One type of criminal that a public humiliation might work par-

ticularly well with are the _____, a lot of
                              youth organization (plural)

whom consider it a badge of honor to be sent to _____
                                                    adjective

detention. And it might not be such a _____ thing
                                          slang for "cool"

in the 'hood to be _____ publicly."
                     same type of punishment (past tense)

27. DUBYA NICKNAMES

Nicknames Granted by President George W. Bush

Tony Blair . . . . Landslide

Barbara Boxer . . . . Ali

Andrew Card . . . . Tangent Man

Dick Cheney . . . . Big Time

Jean Chrétien . . . . Dino (as in Dinosaur)

Maureen Dowd . . . . Cobra

Dianne Feinstein . . . . Frazier

Barney Frank . . . . Sabretooth

Karen Hughes . . . . High Prophet, The Enforcer, Hurricane Karen

Kenneth Lay . . . . Kenny Boy

Colin Powell . . . . Balloonfoot

Condoleezza Rice . . . . Guru

Karl Rove . . . . Turd Blossom

★   ★   ★

Nicknames Granted by President George W. Bush

Tony Blair . . . . _____
bad British food

Barbara Boxer . . . . _____
evil dictator

Andrew Card. . . . . _____ Man
geometry term

Dick Cheney . . . . _____ Time
adjective

Jean Chrétien. . . . . _____
French food

Maureen Dowd . . . . _____
reptile

Dianne Feinstein . . . . _____
same reptile

Barney Frank. . . . . _____
extinct animal

Karen Hughes . . . . _____
female superhero

Kenneth Lay . . . . _____
slang for money

Colin Powell . . . . _____ _____
toy   body part

Condoleezza Rice . . . . _____ Rice
type of rice

Karl Rove. . . . . The _____
medical specialist

28. WHY AMERICA'S GREAT

From an Interview with Former Senator Malcolm Wallop (R), in *Reason*

"The ultimate end is a nation that lies under the concept of the Declaration of Independence. The Declaration of Independence is such an extraordinary statement—it was designed by people skeptical of government, local or national, but in particular national.

"Then the Bill of Rights came along. The idea that government was supposed to be empowered by the people runs right through all those first 10 amendments. And the fascinating thing about that is that it's almost an instruction to stay skeptical. Not to believe the government has no place, but to believe that government's only place is the one that is generated by the will of the people, who are citizens of it, not subjects to it.

"If the Republicans think that by having stated and even achieved most of the Contract that they are therefore entitled to the acceptance and favor of the American voter, they're crazy. We have a long way to go from the Contract to a government that accepts skepticism as part of its rationale, as part of its basis for governing."

★　　　★　　　★

The ultimate end is a nation that lies under the concept of the

_____. It is such a _____ statement—
　　　　religious institution　　　　　　　　　　adjective

it was designed by people skeptical of _____,
　　　　　　　　　　　　　　　　　　　　　　　branch of science

proven or _____.
　　　　　　adjective

Then _____ came along. The idea that
　　　conservative radio/TV personality

the wealthiest _____ Americans were supposed to be em-
　　　　　　　number

powered by the _____ runs right through all
　　　　　　　religious institution

those first _____ broadcasts. And the _____ thing
　　　　　number　　　　　　　　　　　　　　adjective

about that is that it's almost an instruction to stay skeptical.

Not to believe the law of _____ has no place, but to
　　　　　　　　　　　scientific principle

believe that science's only place is in _____, whose citi-
　　　　　　　　　　　　　　　　　　blue state

zens are card-carrying members of _____.
　　　　　　　　　　　　　respected charitable organization

If the _____ Democrats think that by fighting
　　　adjective

_____ and raising _____ they are
　　social problem　　　　　　　　　　　plural noun

therefore entitled to the acceptance and favor of the American

voter, they're crazy. We have a long way to go from the People's

Republic of _____ to a government that accepts
　　　　　famous scientist

the story of _____ as part of its rationale, as part
　　　　　Bible story

of its basis for teaching high school _____.
　　　　　　　　　　　　　　　high school subject

29. FOR IMMEDIATE RELEASE

"In the end, the most productive intelligence on terrorists will come from human spies on the ground. But here, too, the CIA has been woefully slow off the mark. It has an abundance of case officers fluent in French and German and Russian, but, as we now know all too well, few who speak Arabic, Farsi, or Pashto and could slip unnoticed into a street in the Middle East."
—Ted Gup, *Mother Jones,* January/February 2002

"Did President Bush lie to the American people in his State of the Union Message when he said: 'The British government has learned that Saddam Hussein recently sought significant quantities of uranium from Africa'? Technically, no, because 'The statement that he made was indeed accurate,' said National Security Advisor Condoleezza Rice on July 13. 'The British government did say that.' "
—Walter Williams, *The Baltimore Sun,* July 22, 2003

★　　★　　★

FOR IMMEDIATE RELEASE

Office of the Press Secretary

The White House would like to clarify its earlier statement regarding _____ and _____ harboring weapons
　　　　　　　　evil leader　　　　　　　country

of mass destruction, which, according to the October report by

the _____, is now known to be _____. Reports
　　government agency　　　　　　　　　　　adjective

furnished to the _____ by intelligence oper-

intelligence agency

atives from _____ reported correctly

traditional U.S. ally opposed to the war in Iraq

that _____ *was* harboring WMDs. However,

country from first sentence

due to the shortage of _____-speaking

language spoken in above U.S. allied country

translators at the _____ led the agency to report

same intelligence agency

incorrectly that _____ was harboring weapons of mass

above leader

destruction. When correctly translated, however, the WMDs

referred to in the _____ report were actually

same allied country (adjective)*

_____ of _____,

plural noun starting with "w"   adjective starting with "m"

_____. Translation errors

noun beginning with "d," ending in -tion

were also responsible for the confusion about our search

for 'yellowcake,' which was actually a hunt for the

_____ _____ in

superlative   bakery item common in country from first sentence

_____, not for nuclear _____.

same country   plural noun

We sincerely apologize to the government of _____

ally

for the misunderstanding.

Thank you.

_____

*E.g., *Swiss, German.*

30. MOTHER OF THE YEAR

"What I'm hearing, which is sort of scary, is they all want to stay in Texas. Everyone is overwhelmed by the hospitality. And so many of the people in the arena here, you know, were underprivileged anyway, so this is working very well for them."

—Barbara Bush, referring to Hurricane Katrina evacuees
at the Houston Astrodome, September 7, 2005

★   ★   ★

Note to Players

First choose a _____. *Use that*
country with really bad regime propped up by the U.S.

same country each time you're asked for information about

_____ *in the MadLiberal below.*
same country

First _____ Barbara Bush visited the _____
female royal   natural disaster

evacuees at the _____ Stadium in
notorious person from same country (full name)*

_____ today, proving that her compassion and
capital of same country

empathy are in top form. "What I'm hearing, which is sort of

_____, is that they all want to stay in _____.
adjective   capital of same country

Everyone is overwhelmed by the _____.
something same country is known for (noun)

And so many of the _____ in the arena,
common job in same country (plural)

here, you know, were _____ anyway, so this
adjective beginning with un-

is working very well for them."

   Later, during an impromptu prayer session, Mrs. Bush let

some of the evacuees touch the hem of her garment with their

_____ before making the sign of the _____
body part (plural)   an icon

and leaving.

_____

*If you can't think of one, substitute the deceased dictator of your choice.

31. ON THE ROAD TO THE WHITE HOUSE—MADLIBERALS EDITION!

MadLiberals everywhere can find many amusing and tasteful must-have gift items at The White House Gift Shop, available online at www.whitehousegiftshop.com. They're all here: The Air Force One Play Set ($22 large, $13 small), The George W. Bush Beanie-Bear ($10), even Presidential Seal Bath Towels (navy blue, heavy-weight, $28). Dry off in style!

Our favorite is the On the Road to the White House board game (ages 8 and up), which can be yours for $30.

On the next page you can help us create the rules for a game we'd love to see: On the Road to the White House—MadLiberals Edition!

★   ★   ★

For 2 or More Players

Setup: One player starts with _____ of dollars. The
                                    very large number

other player(s) usually has (have) _____ of dollars,
                                    much lower number

but sometimes, they have the same amount.

The Play: Each player must perform four actions:

1. Pander to _____. Promise to "actively
                special interest group

    _____," and to "feel their _____."
         verb   emotion

2. Pander to _____. Make sure to exchange
                    industry

    _____ support for _____ donations.
         adjective   adjective

3. Pander to the media. Make sure you wear _____
                                              article of clothing (plural)

    that look good on television. Your wife should bake

    _____ and share the recipe. Kiss a lot
         all-American food

    of _____.
         noun (plural)

4. Pander to your party. Meet with _____.
                                      extreme member of a political party

    Pander. Then deny it.

32. NUCLEAR POWER

*Due to its proximity to the world's financial center and the severe conse-
quences to public health, the environment and the economy that would
result from a major accident or terrorist attack, Indian Point is a nuclear
power plant that deserves special attention. Twenty million people live
within a 50-mile radius of the plant—the highest population density
within 50 miles of any nuclear power plant in the United States. A terrorist attack on either of Indian Point's two reactors or their spent fuel pools,
or a large-scale accident, could render much of the tristate area uninhabitable and indefinitely contaminate the watershed that supplies drinking water to nine million people in the region. That the plant sits atop an
active fault line, daily destroys significant amounts of Hudson River
aquatic life and has abysmal security, operations and safety records only
compounds the arguments for closure.*

SOURCE: Lisa Rainwater van Suntum, director, Riverkeeper's Indian Point Campaign.
From *PR Watch,* Vol. 12, No. 1, First Quarter 2005.

Maybe They'd Shut One Down If . . .

Due to its proximity to the world's _____
sport popular with the rich

center and the severe consequences to public _____,
something public

_____, and _____ that
something all-American ultra-conservative media outlet

would result from a major _____ accident or
type of accident

_____ attack, _____ is a nuclear power
      _{type of attack}   _{horror movie}

plant that deserves special attention. _____
                  _{Number between one and ten}

Republicans live within a 50-mile radius of the plant—the

highest _____ density within 50 miles of any
        _{make of luxury car}

nuclear power plant in the United States. A _____
                _{same type of attack}

on either of _____'s two reactors or their
         _{same horror movie}

_____ _____ pools, or a large-scale
   _{adjective}   _{spa treatment}

_____ rally, could render much of the tri-
     _{liberal cause}

state area uninhabitable and indefinitely contaminate the water-

shed that supplies drinking water to nine million members of

_____ in the region. That the plant sits atop
  _{group that supports Bush}

an active _____, daily destroys significant
       _{place where the wealthy gather}

amounts of _____, and has abysmal security
       _{alcoholic beverage}

operations and _____ only compound the
        _{safety item (plural)*}

arguments for closure.

---

*E.g., *helmet.*

33. ARE YOU TOUCHING YOURSELF?

PLAY WITH YOURSELF!

Use this handy table to fill in the blanks used on the next page:

_____
common bad habit

_____
famous blind person

_____
same common bad habit (practitioner)*

_____
vice or perversion

_____
dead rock star

_____
fatal health problem

_____
embarrassing minor health problem

_____
percentage

_____
form of punishment

_____

*E.g., *nose picker, liar, Republican voter,* etc.

Please read this before you consider _____.
common bad habit

1. _____ is dangerous. There are many cases of
Same common habit
   people engaging in this habit and going blind. While he
   was/is embarrassed to state it publicly, _____
   famous blind person
   was/has been a lifelong _____.
   same common habit practitioner*

2. _____ is a starter sin. Virtually everyone who
Same common habit
   engages in _____ engaged in _____
   vice or perversion   same common habit
   before they took up _____.
   same vice or perversion

3. _____ leads to eternal damnation. If you don't
Same common habit
   believe us, just ask the spirit of _____.
   dead rock star

4. _____ leads to other health problems.
Same common habit
   Recent scientific evidence points to a connection between
   _____ and _____ and occasionally
   same common habit   fatal health problem
   _____.
   embarrassing minor health problem

5. And finally, _____ helps the terrorists.
   same common habit
   _____ of all al-Qaeda members captured
   Percentage
   have confessed, after prolonged _____, that
   form of punishment
   they obtained useful information about our vulnerabilities
   from _____.
   same common habit practitioner (plural)

---

*E.g., *nose picker, liar, Republican voter,* etc.

34. ETHICS RULES

"First of all, I appreciate everyone who is working so hard for the American people and President Bush's administration. That applies to everyone, whether they're a political appointee or they've been a wonderful career employee."

—Andy Card, Not-Yet-Indicted Coconspirator
and Former White House Chief of Staff

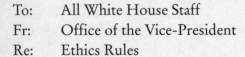

To: All White House Staff
Fr: Office of the Vice-President
Re: Ethics Rules

As you know, _____ reported yesterday that
                        snarky website

_____ members of the White House staff were discovered
    number

stealing _____ from the _____
         common household item (plural)   room in your house

closet in the White House. This morning's _____
                                                  newspaper

disclosed—equally without foundation—that the President of

_____ gave thirteen million _____ to
    obscure country   units of foreign currency

the _____ Foundation for the Advancement of
          adjective

Liberal Ideas (a conservative think tank), _____
                                                  adverb

with the expectation of arranging a meeting with me in the

_____ Office. Accordingly, I have ordered that all
    shape

White House staff receive a _____ course on proper
                                  adjective
ethical behavior when dealing with members of the media.

Despite the fact that these allegations are _____
                                                      adverb
_____, they serve as a reminder that whatever
          adjective
you _____ at the White House stays at the White
        one of five senses
House. Official Government ethics rules are the _____
                                                        adjective
acceptable standard of conduct. In other words, the rules
_____ what is wrong, not what is _____.
        verb   adjective
Truly ethical conduct means _____ less than
                                  verb ending in -ing
the law allows and more than the law requires.

When in doubt, ask yourself: "What would _____
                                              former Republican President
do?"

                              Yours,
                              Richard B. Cheney

cc: Karl Rove, Head of the Ethics Committee
       Scooter Libby, Honorary Chair

bcc: (leaked) _____
                  well-known journalist

35. IAO NEEDS MORE INFO, COVER LETTER

The Former Official Logo*

The Information Awareness Office and its Total Information Awareness (TIA) program, created in the wake of 9/11, was given a $200 million budget to create computer dossiers on 300 million Americans. In February 2003, under Congressional scrutiny and threatened with closure, the IAO posted the following statement on its website:

> "Because the IAO logo has become a lightning rod and is need-
> lessly diverting time and attention from the critical tasks of exe-
> cuting that office's mission effectively and openly, we have
> decided to discontinue the use of the original logo."

The IAO itself was ordered closed later that year. According to the *National Journal,* however, several TIA projects continue to be funded by other agencies.

---

*IAO logo merchandise is available for sale at buyathongforfreedom.com. Proceeds benefit the ACLU.

Dear _____,

As a patriotic citizen of _____, I'm sure that
you would like to help the United States keep our country safe

from _____ and _____
terrorists. Due to a _____ error, our wiretaps
of your recent conversations are   incomplete.
We hope that you can fill in the missing _____
phrases and return this form to us in the attached, self-

addressed envelope.

I know that I speak for all of us here at the Information Aware-

ness Office when I thank you for your swift cooperation. Or

else. Don't even ask. We mean it.

Yours,

_____
Director, Information Awareness Office

cc: Dick Cheney

36. OXYMORON 1: REPUBLICAN ENVIRONMENTALISTS

MISSION STATEMENT

Like the great GOP President, Theodore Roosevelt, we are Republicans who believe conservation benefits all Americans. The Council of Republicans for Environmental Advocacy (CREA) is committed to preserving America's natural resources, air, water, and scenic beauty for future generations. CREA's mission is to foster environmental protection by promoting fair, community-based solutions to environmental challenges, highlighting Republican environmental accomplishments and building on our Republican tradition of conservation.

SOURCE: www.crea-online.org

✶   ✶   ✶

When Gale was younger, she decided to become a _____
                                                        adjective
environmentalist. First, she found a pristine _____
                                                       body of water
and decided to make it clean by adding a full bottle of

_____. Disappointed that the water wasn't
      brand of cleaning fluid

_____ enough, she added an entire case.
   adjective

Next, Gale focused on the _____ animal
                                  pejorative adjective
droppings near her house. Unhappy with the untidiness, she

took several boxes of _____ and spread them
_____ kind of poison

around. All of the _____ disappeared, which made
_____ animal (plural)

Gale _____. She persevered.
_____ emotion

"If _____ had wanted the air to smell like _____
_____ deity _____ plant (plural)

he would have created them!" Determined to clean up the air,

Gale burned down her neighbor's expensive _____.
_____ noun

Gale Norton would grow to become Secretary of the Inte-

rior. When she met _____ during a tour
_____ stupid Hollywood starlet

of the White House, the starlet said, "Oh, I love what you've

done with the inside of the White House!" The two have been

friends ever since, and Ms. _____ now regu-
_____ last name of same starlet

larly appears in Public Service Announcements for the DOI,

posing with _____ and expressing her sup-
_____ endangered species

port for _____ in _____.
_____ verb ending in -ing _____ National Park

37. THEY'RE SPYING ON US

President Bush signed a secret order in 2002 authorizing the National Security Agency to eavesdrop on U.S. citizens and foreign nationals in the United States, despite previous legal prohibitions against such domestic spying.

—*Washington Post,* December 16, 2005

"There are multiple checks and balances to make sure what we're doing is targeting . . . international phone calls of terrorists, not the conversations between two families coordinating a family vacation."

— White House spokesman Dan Bartlett

✶   ✶   ✶

From Telephone Surveillance Transcript

GIRL: This trip to _____ is going to be the
                                     vacation destination

bomb!

FRIEND: I made a music mix for us to bring on the plane.

I downloaded that new song by The _____
                                         verb ending with -ing

_____.
weapon (plural)

GIRL: Which one, "Bloody _____"?
                                      noun

I would kill to have the whole album! They are so

_____. We'll have to keep the volume
            adjective

down while on the plane; that one's pretty explosive.

FRIEND: I wish my _____ didn't have to come with us.

male family member

He is so _____. He always hijacks the

insulting adjective

conversation.

GIRL: Does he have to come? It's not like anyone's holding a

gun to his _____.

body part

FRIEND: Yeah, but he's dying to go visit an old _____

sport

friend over there, who he says he's going to kill in a

game.

GIRL: Oh well. I can't believe the flight is so early in the

morning, though. I'm going to totally crash at the

hotel.

Scooter
Pls get back to NSA
on this. OK to have
_____ -pay
cartoon character
these two evildoers
a visit.   —Dick

38. WHITE HOUSE BIBLE STUDY

Every day, twenty-five to fifty White House staffers gather for Bible study classes. "Our governments must not fear faith," George W. Bush said. "We must welcome faith in our society."

Richard Nixon, a Quaker, also held Bible classes at the White House.

When Goliath faced _____, it was a _____
                    biblical character   sporting event

between _____ and _____. This lesson also
              a virtue   a sin

applies to world affairs. When the United States invades a

_____ country like _____, we are sending a
      adjective   country

clear message: "_____." The
                        one of the Ten Commandments

_____ of _____ soon realizes the wisdom
      job title   same country

of the old saying "_____."
                                          proverb

_____ is not neutral in the ways of war, and has chosen
    Greek god

our country to lead a mission in pursuit of _____.
                                                 natural resource

We must have faith in our leaders just as we have faith in

_____ that we are _____
        same Greek god   verb ending in -ing

a divine _____ toward righteousness.
                  noun

Let us close with a(n) _____ of silence, followed
                            period of time

by _____ leading us in the singing of
          White House staff member

_____.
        patriotic song

39. SURVIVAL GUIDE FOR SENIORS

It began as a novelty: grannies riding buses to Canada in search of cheaper medicines. But today, that search has mushroomed into a cross-border war that pits desperate consumers and defiant state and local governments against the powerful pharmaceutical industry and the Bush administration.

From just a few million dollars a year in 2000, the importation of price-controlled drugs from Canada has grown to a projected $800 million this year and shows no signs of letting up.

The Bush administration, echoing the arguments of drugmakers, is fighting the medicine trade from Canada and elsewhere as illegal and unsafe . . .

The border war is being driven by a rapid rise in the cost of medications and the frustration of one in four U.S. seniors who have no drug coverage.

SOURCE: *USA Today,* October 7, 2003

★　　　★　　　★

The _____ _____
type of weather (adjective)　　　　　　　　type of tree

Retirement Community has released the following memo for its

residents, in light of recent Social Security reform:

Is money tight? Brush off that resumé! Finding a job as a

_____ may be a _____ way
minimum-wage job (noun)　　　　　　　　　adjective

to ease into a working retirement.

Go over your Medicare plan options. You might ask a family

member or _____ to help explain them to you.
famous living scientist

If you'd like to do it yourself, learning _____
computer program

will help, as will an advanced degree in _____.
field of mathematics

Homemade remedies are an affordable alternative to prescrip-

tion drugs. Crushing up _____ root into your
animal

_____ may alleviate _____.
food　　　　　　　　　　　　　　　　ailment

Alternately, you can find a _____ to
mode of transportation

_____, where you have access to _____
country　　　　　　　　　　　　　　　　　　adjective

prescription drugs.

Did we mention _____? It's packed with nutri-
brand of cat food

tients and has been keeping _____ strong for years.
cat name

40. HOW TO COMBAT DECLINING POLL NUMBERS

Despite the occasional groundswell of popular support during times of crisis, Bush's approval ratings have declined steadily since his election in 2000. Below is a simplified version of a chart tracking data from several polling organizations, compiled and regularly updated by Professor Steven Ruggles of the University of Minnesota. The original can be viewed at http://www.hist.umn.edu/~ruggles/Approval.htm.

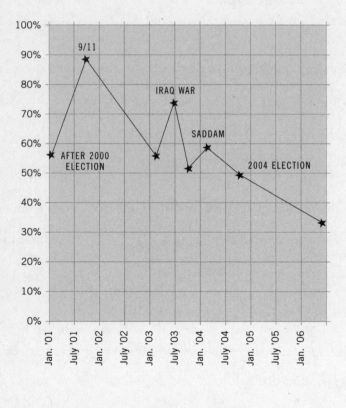

Ways of Combating Declining Poll Numbers

1. Ban gay _____, making the practice
   celebration (plural)
   unconstitutional.

2. Repeal the _____ tax.
   luxury brand

3. Announce the arrest in _____ of the _____
   country   ordinal number
   Al Qaeda second-in-command to be captured this year.

4. Condemn all the declining moral values evidenced on

   _____ and _____. Encour-
   reality show   sitcom
   age the American people to focus on more _____
   noun
   friendly media like _____.
   right-wing or conservative TV/radio show or publication

5. Introduce a constitutional amendment that makes it pun-

   ishable by _____ to _____
   punishment   verb
   the American flag.

6. Shift focus to the _____ immigration problem.
   nationality
   Propose building a _____-foot _____ around
   number   noun
   the United States and deploy troops to the border to help

   keep the _____ from _____
   same nationality   verb ending in -ing
   across.

Don't Just Get Mad

We set out to create a funny book, a book that would allow us to let off some steam. After all, we *need* a good laugh. As this book goes to press, the Bush administration seems more out of control than ever. The President's approval ratings are at an all-time low, Iraq is tilting ever closer toward all-out civil war, two new conservative justices have joined the Supreme Court and abortion rights are again under fire. . . .

What's happening to America is serious business, and MadLiberals need to do more than get mad. So buy lots of copies, and give them to your friends. Get together with other MadLiberals, fill in the blanks, and have some laughs. And when you're done wiping the tears of mirth from your _____, remember that the

                    body part (plural)

people around the living room are exactly the ones who can make a difference.

So get mad, liberals—and then get noisy. Write letters, sign petitions, host events, post on your blog, donate money to the organizations and candidates you believe in. And vote—early, often, and liberal. We need a big victory party in November.

BECOME A MADLIBERAL

Getting in the MadLiberals groove? We'd love to hear from you. You can submit your own fill-in-the-blanks pages for our next volume. Visit www.madliberals.org for details.

About the Authors

The MadLiberals is a group of _____ liberal writers,

adverb

editors, and _____ dedicated to

member of profession (plural)

raising public awareness of the _____ policies of

adjective

the Bush administration, and to supporting the election of

candidates who oppose them. They live in _____.

blue state

    For information about what you can do to help, visit

our website at www.madliberals.org.

    _____ percent of the proceeds from this book

Very small number

will be donated to _____

political party we'd like to see in the White House (adjective)

candidates, to help preserve _____

endangered civil liberty

and to support other causes that need more help than ever under the current administration. (Actually, we'll be donating more than that, but if you're a _____ liberal

_{adjective}

like us, you probably wouldn't believe us anyway.)

We hope you'll donate generously, too.

✸   ✸   ✸

WANT TO JOIN THE MADLIBERALS TEAM?

We welcome the submission of more fill-in-the-blanks pages like the ones you've enjoyed in this book for use in future volumes. Find out more at www.madliberals.org.

ACKNOWLEDGMENTS

The MadLiberals would like to thank their literary agent, Stuart Krichevsky; his madly liberal colleagues Shana Cohen and Elizabeth Kellermeyer; Robin Dellabough, for her friendship and inspiration; and everyone who offered their support, contributions, and good humor to the cause—you know who you are.